WHERE'S MY PEG?

WAYLAND

NEW EXPERIENCES

I Want That Room! Moving house
I'm Still Important! A new baby
Open Wide! My first trip to the dentist
Where's My Peg? My first day at school

First published in 1999 by Wayland Publishers Ltd.
This edition published in 2007 by Wayland,
an imprint of Hachette Children's Books
© Copyright 1999 Wayland
All rights reserved

Editor: Jason Hook
Designer: Tessa Barwick
Cover Designer: Caroline Martin

British Library Cataloguing in Publication Data
Green, Jen, 1955–
Where's my peg?: my first day at school. – (New experiences)
1. First day of school – Juvenile literature
I. Title II. Gordon, Mike, 1948–
371
ISBN 978 0 7502 5283 6

Printed and bound in China

Hachette Children's Books
338 Euston Road, London NW1 3BH

For Joseph with love, and with thanks to Jamie.

WHERE'S MY PEG?

My first day at school

Written by Jen Green

Illustrated by Mike Gordon

WAYLAND

Today I woke up early. The big day was here at last – my first day at school.

At breakfast, I felt excited but a bit worried. 'Will I know anyone there?' I asked Mum. 'What if I get lost?'

Mum gave me a big hug. 'Sonia from the next road is starting today, too,' she said.

Dad said: 'Remember, if you need anything just ask.'

7

After breakfast, Dad waved us goodbye. Mum and I walked to school with Sonia and her dad.

There were lots of children playing
in the playground. I felt shy.

A grown-up came over. She said,
'I'm your teacher, Mrs Taylor. We met
when you came in for storytime.'

She called a big boy over. 'Sam will show you your peg, where you can put your coat.'

This is Sam.

All the pegs had pictures.
My peg had a lion.

Sam showed me
the toilets, and the sinks
where you wash your hands.

Sam showed us the classroom. There was a dressing-up box, a playhouse, a computer, a book corner, and a guinea pig called Eric.

Everyone was busy doing something. Sonia built a tower with bricks.

I watched, and then I joined in.

Afterwards a girl
called Rosie fed Eric
while I stroked him.

17

At breaktime we had a drink and a biscuit. Then we went outside.

It was like nursery, but there were more children. Sonia and I played near another teacher, Mrs Thomas.

19

After break we went to the hall
and sang songs with Mr Griffiths.
It was very noisy.

Then we went back to our class.
Mrs Taylor was busy, so I looked
at a book with Sam.

Before lunch we washed our hands.
I had fish, peas and potatoes for
lunch. Mrs Taylor had the same.

At playtime, I played in the
sandpit with Mike and Mary.

After lunch I painted a picture of our dog, Sandy. I asked Mrs Taylor for some help.

She wrote down his name and I copied the letters.

'Come on, everyone,
it's time to tidy up,'
said Mrs Taylor.

We sat on a mat while Mrs Taylor read to us. Then I saw Mum at the door. It was time to go home already!

'Mum, I painted a picture of Sandy,' I told her. 'Mrs Taylor liked it.'

'What will you do tomorrow?'
Mum asked. I didn't know, but
I was already excited about my
second day at school.

Notes for parents and teachers

This book introduces children to the new experience of going to school. Parents or teachers may find it useful to stop and discuss issues as they come up.

Starting school is a major new experience for a child. Challenges include meeting many new children and a variety of adults, being part of a large group and sharing adult attention, and the unfamiliar timetable of the school day. This book introduces some of the activities that go on in classrooms.

To prepare your child for school, visit school with him or her on several occasions. Make sure your child has met his or her teacher, and is familiar with the layout of the classroom and toilets. If possible, meet up with other children who are starting school at the same time, and arrange to link up with them on the way to school.

Your child may feel apprehensive about starting school. Be honest and admit that some things will seem strange at first. Make sure your child knows to ask if he or she needs to use the toilet.

Encourage your child to look forward to the new experience. Before the first day, mark all items of clothing with your child's name, and make sure clothes can be managed independently.

Children who have started school might like to tell the story of their own first day, using the book as a framework. How did their own experiences differ from those described in the book? Their stories could be put together to make a class book entitled 'Our first day at school'. Reread the story together, encouraging children to take the roles of the different characters.

The experience of starting school introduces children to many unfamiliar words, including: class, classroom, lesson, breaktime, lunchbox, playtime, playground, assembly, dinner lady, head teacher. Make a list of new words and discuss what they mean.

Use this book for teaching literacy

This book can help you in the literacy hour in the following ways:

- ✓ Children can write simple stories linked to personal experience, using the language of the text in this book as a model for their own writing. (Year 1, Term 3: Non-fiction writing composition.)

- ✓ Children can look through the book and try to locate verbs with past and present tense endings. (Year 1, Term 3: Word recognition, graphic knowledge and spelling.)

- ✓ The use of speech bubbles shows a different way of presenting text. (Year 2, Term 2: Sentence construction and punctuation.)

Books to read

Billy and the Big New School by Catherine and Laurence Anholt (Orchard Books, 2004). Billy was excited but worried about starting at the big school. What if he got lost, or couldn't tie his new shoes with the difficult laces?

Going to School by Anne Civardi and Stephen Cartwright (Usborne Publishing, 2005). Polly and Percy Peach and their friend Millie are starting school together. Percy's pet gerbil Sidney helps the day go well.

A Day in the Life of a Teacher by Carol Watson (Franklin Watts, 2001). Mrs Harvey is a primary school teacher. The book follows her through the course of a busy day at school, as she helps her class and plans a concert for the end of term.